photo guides

Capturing
Easter Island

Planning and executing great travel photography

James Dugan

Reader bonuses

As a thank you to readers of this guide, we have some bonuses to help you plan and execute a great travel photography trip to Easter Island:

- **Free eBook "Managing your camera equipment and images"** - This eBook is packed with practical tips on ensuring that you get the best performance out of your cameras, and how to manage your images when you are on the ground.

- **Access to the photos in the guide** - You can now get access to large-size versions of all of the images found in the guide.

- **How-to guide for Google Maps list** - Step-by-step (with screenshots) guide to creating a custom Google Maps list. We've also included access to the Google Maps list that we've used for Easter Island as well!

For your free bonuses, head over to

walkaboutphotoguides.com/easterisland/guidebonus/

About this guide

Our guides help you maximise your time on the ground to get a great set of photos. This guide walks you through the planning and logistics that go into a productive and enjoyable trip to take photos in Easter Island.

Taking a trip with the express intention of taking photos can be different to a regular trip in a few important ways. The biggest difference is chasing the best light for your subjects – good light is often the secret sauce to capturing a compelling image.

Structure your visits to specific locations to coincide with the best light conditions. This means being able to be flexible with your schedule, particularly if you have to work with variable weather conditions.

Most of all, take time to appreciate your surroundings.

May you have fantastic light, full camera batteries, and no space left on your memory cards at the end!

Map legends

Throughout the guide, you will see these symbols in maps and some other parts as well. We've compiled it here for your easy reference.

 Airport   Cave   Cemetery

 Church   Monument   Museum

 Photo opportunity   Ruins   Viewpoint

Frequently asked questions

The Frequently Asked Questions (FAQ) below allow you to dive straight into the guide.

Q: Where is the information about hotels, bars, restaurants, and shopping found in other travel guides?

A: Our guides are focused on providing you with the information you need to hit the ground and take good photos. We emphasise this with detailed maps and diagrams, photos, camera settings, and lots of logistical information. This is where we have invested our time through research and boots on the ground.

Being perfectly honest - hotels, bars, restaurants, and shopping options change fairly often, and it is a huge effort keeping this information current. We trust that our readers are comfortable with making their accommodation bookings online through aggregators, as well as reading up-to-date reviews for bars and restaurants.

And we assume that if you're already lugging all of your photography gear, there's not much room left for the shopping!

Q: How does this guide differ from a photography tour?

A: Photography tours are a fantastic way to have a local photographer show you about the island and share with you their secret shooting spots. They are also able to provide you with on-the-spot tips and advice to improve the quality of your photos taken. Tour guides can help with translation as required. Lastly, having others around, particularly a local, can allay fears of attracting unwanted attention.

However, you do need to pay for the photographer's valuable time. You'll also need to book them in advance and agree a time that works for both of you (assuming you don't have to join a small group where the time will be dictated already). Hopefully the weather conditions are favourable during your booking!

Our guides provide much of this knowledge and insight whilst allowing you to be flexible with your time and allow for potentially changing weather conditions.

If possible, consider both a photo tour and our guide as they are natural complements.

Table of contents

Welcome to
Easter Island

aster Island (English), Isla de Pascua (Spanish), or Rapa ui (local language), is one of the remotest places on arth. Renowned around the world for their "head" tatues, known as *moai*, the island has long been a draw ard for intrepid travellers.

he combination of the isolation, amazing *moai*, and reeless landscape make Easter Island an unforgettable photographic experience. If you tire of taking photos and exploring, the island is also famous for its surfing and diving options.

105mm, f/11, ISO 200, 1/320 sec
FF camera

1.01 The seven *moai* found at Ahu Akivi are unusual as they face towards the sea.

 **90mm, f/11, ISO 50, 0.4 sec
FF camera**

1.02 Having humans in front of the 15 *moai* of Ahu Tongariki at sunrise gives a sense of scale.

Photo themes

It is possible to take in the key sites of Easter Island in a couple of days, assuming that you get great weather (and light). Sunrises are the main logistical challenge, largely down to how good you are at getting up before it's light.

The reality is that the majority of people will only make one trip to Easter Island in their life. To help maximise opportunities to get great photos in a short space of time, here are the highlight photo themes that draw travel photographers here.

Although the island is small and easily traversed (particularly by car), it does make sense to plan your day's itinerary around where you want to be for sunset. This way you don't end up criss-crossing the island as you chase the setting sun.

Sunrises

Sunrises on Easter Island can be amazing at any time, however there's a degree of luck in getting a sunrise that isn't affected in some way by cloud cover. This means multiple trips to capture the sunrise, if possible. Stand-out sunrise locations include:

- **Ahu Tongariki** (page 20) - The most photographed sunrise location on Easter Island actually faces towards the sun. Silhouettes are the name of the game here, and positioning yourself with your tripod in the field to the West is the best place to start.

- **Ahu Tahai** (page 17) - A sunrise location that is walking distance from your accommodation sounds good, right? Here you can watch the sun slowly sweep across the *moai*, including catching the eye of the lone *moai* of Ahu Ko Te Riku.

- **Ma'unga Terevaka (page 40)** - Offering panoramic views across the island, you'll need to allow an hour to hike up to be in position for the sunrise.

75mm, f/11, ISO 50, 1/13 sec
FF camera

1.03 Watching sunrise over the five *moai* of Ahu Vai Uri, the centrepiece of the Ahu Tahai area.

Sunsets

Sunsets on Easter Island don't quite have the same wow factor as sunrises, however don't head for dinner too early. There are a couple of stand-out sunset locations that are worth being in position for:

- **Ahu Tahai (page 17)** - You will be amongst company, as this site is a popular picnic destination to watch the sunset as well.

- **Anakena (page 24)** - Facing the *moai*, the sun will now be to your back towards the end of the day. This allows for shadow-free and pleasing images of the faces of the *moai*.

Giant heads (Moai)

The *moai* (page 14) are most likely the reason that you're heading to Easter Island. There are almost 900 that have been identified, however here are the best places to go to photograph the iconic statues:

- **Ahu Akivi (page 16)** - The most prominent inland site, the six *moai* here are all still in relatively good condition.

- **Ahu Ko Te Riku (page 18)** - Probably the best preserved *moai* to be found outdoors, complete with *pukao* and bright white eyes.

- **Ahu Tongariki (page 20)** - Featuring the largest *ahu* on the island, there are 15 *moai* standing proudly with their backs to the sea.

- **Rano Raraku (page 30)** - Easter Island's *moai* factory, there are more statues here than anywhere else on the island in all shapes and sizes.

105mm, f/11, ISO 200, 1/250 sec
FF camera

1.04 Ahu Tongariki and its 15 *moai* with their backs to the sea, taken from Rano Raraku.

Rapa Nui National Park

apa Nui National Park is a wildlife area whose main
oal is to protect the culture and the legacy of the
ative people of Rapa Nui. The island was declared a
NESCO World Heritage Site in 1996, and restoration
ork is ongoing to preserve the *moai*. The park is under
e supervision of the local Ma'u Henua Polynesian
digenous community, after the Chilean government
eded responsibility for the park's management.

Tip

If you are approaching closing time, carry a
telephoto lens with you. You are able to see all
of the sites from nearby roads / fences, even if
the viewing angles may not be as great.

Logistics

Tickets and opening times

Top sites – Ahu Akivi, Anakena, Orongo ceremonial
village, Rano Raraku

🕐 Monday and Wednesday: 09:30 - 20:00
Thursday to Sunday, Tuesday: 09:00 - 20:00

Other park sites

🕐 Monday and Wednesday: 09:30 - 18:00.
Thursday to Sunday, Tuesday: 09:00 - 18:00

General entry

🎟 Refer to the section on Rapa Nui National Park
access (page 58).

 70mm, f/8, ISO 200, 1/400 sec
CF 1.5x camera
1.05 A lone *moai* greets visitors to Ahu Tongariki as
you enter from the carpark on the South.

50mm, f/11, ISO 200, 1/250 sec
FF camera

1.06 Rano Raraku viewed from the entrance shows why it is considered the *moai* graveyard.

Easter Island statues

The Easter Island statues have long fascinated historians, archaeologists, ethnographers, and even visitors. There is consensus as to the purpose of the statues, however there is still debate as to whether the islanders' obsession with their creation caused irreversible environmental impact.

Ahu (platforms)

In the Rapa Nui language, the word "ahu" refers to the stone that acts as a support base for a *moai*. An average ahu measures around 1.20 metres tall. The *ahu* is considered a sacred ceremonial place whose job is to support the *moai*. The *ahu* are found along the coastlines of the island, with the main exception of Ahu Akivi (page 16). Clans typically had their own ahu, which is why it is common to find remains of villages nearby an *ahu*.

The largest ahu on Easter Island can be found at Ahu Tongariki (page 20), complete with 15 restored *moai*.

Warning

Do not walk on the ahu! This is seen as deeply disrespectful to the inhabitants of Rapa Nui, and will result in fines and / or prosecution. Note that many *ahu* are roped / fenced off as a further visual reminder to keep your distance.

M Rano Raraku

N Ana Kai Tangata

O Ana Hue Neru

P Ana Kakenga

Q Ana Te Pahu

R Ana Te Pora

S Ma'unga Terevaka

T Poike

G Ahu Te Peu

H Ahu Te Pito Kura

I Ahu Tongariki

J Ahu Vinapu

K Orongo
   ceremonial village

L Papa Vaka

A Airport

B Ahu Akahanga

C Ahu Akivi

D Ahu Huri a Urenga

E Anakena

F Ahu Tahai

MAP 1.1   Easter Island

© OPENSTREETMAP CONTRIBUTORS

Moai

1.07

100mm, f/11, ISO 125, 1/250 sec
FF camera

Humans create scale. They also tend to want to view the *moai* up-close, so be patient.

> **#** #easterislandhead, #easterislandheads, #easterislandmoai, #moai, #moais, #moai, #moaï

The *moai* are monolithic statues carved by the inhabitants of Easter Island between the 12th and 17th centuries CE, with almost 900 having been identified over the years. They represent the deified ancestors of the islanders, believed to be guarding the land and their descendants.

Contrary to popular belief, the *moai* are not simply the heads of statues with their bodies buried in the ground. The heads of the *moai* are larger than their bodies, around 3/8 of the total size. This stems from the Polynesian belief in the importance of the head. Although the heads look similar, the arms are carved in various positions in the body.

The *moai* are mostly made from tuff, a compressed volcanic ash, but there are also *moai* that were made of basalt, trachyte, and red scoria, a very light rock found a Puna Pau.

Pukao

The *pukao* is a topknot or headdress that indicates the status of the *moai*. According to Polynesian tradition, only the chieftain wears a *pukao*. That's because they believe that a person's *mana* (power) is preserved in the hair. This feature was added in the more recent *moai*, and is made from red scoria found at Puna Pau (page 41). The people of Rapa Nui believe that the colour red signifies nobility.

75mm, f/11, ISO 400, 1/320 sec
FF camera

1.08 The early morning sun on the backs of the 15 *moai* ion the huge *ahu* at Ahu Tongariki.

Top sites to visit

s has been mentioned elsewhere, Easter Island can be overed in a relatively short number of days. If you're naking your way out so far, hopefully you are giving ourself a few days to take it all in and allowing for variable light conditions. The top sites to visit in Rapa Nui National Park (well, Easter Island) often warrant a return visit at a different time of day.

The two exceptions are Orongo ceremonial village (page 27) and Rano Raraku (page 30), where you're only permitted to enter once using your Park access. Where possible, structure your itinerary around being in position at these two sites at the optimal time of day for great photos (see details for each site).

Lastly, don't dismiss the other sites that are described in this guide. You should visit as many as you are able to squeeze in.

80mm, f/11, ISO 250, 1/200 sec
FF camera

1.09 Shadows slowly disappearing in the morning sun at Ahu Tahai (Ahu Vai Uri here).

Ahu Akivi

Ahu Akivi, located at the southwest side of Maunga Terevaka, was constructed during the 16th century. Unusual for *moai*, the seven identical statues are located inland, and all face towards the sea (the usual custom is to have backs to the sea). Local legend explains that this is to please the sea so that navigators had safe passage.

The *moai* sit atop a 70-metre *ahu* and have been positioned such that they face sunset during the equinoxes, making the site of astrological significance.

45mm, f/11, ISO 200, 4 sec
FF camera

1.10   Using a Neutral Density (ND) filter for a daytime long-exposure shot to create drama.

135mm, f/8, ISO 200, 1/640 sec
CF 1.5x camera

1.11   Using a telephoto zoom for the *moai* statues helps compress the detail in the image.

Ahu Tahai area

1.12

24mm, f/11, ISO 200, 30 sec
FF camera

A 10-stop ND filter allowed a long-exposure shot which captured the pink in the clouds.

#ahutahai, #ahuvaiuri, #ahukoteriku, #ahutahaiisladepascua

Probably one of the most photographed locations on Easter Island, Ahu Tahai is walking distance from Hanga Roa. This makes it a great sunrise and sunset location, particularly if you're unsure about the weather conditions. The site itself contains many archaeological points of interest including the remains of a village replete with *hare paenga* (boat houses) and rather large stone *hare moa* (chicken coops).

The main point of attraction is definitely the three *ahu* and their *moai*.

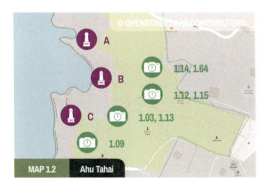

MAP 1.2   Ahu Tahai

    A   Ahu Ko Te Riku

    B   Ahu Tahai

    C   Ahu Vai Uri

70mm, f/8, ISO 160, 1/200 sec
FF camera

1.13 Ahu Tahai (mid-ground) and Ahu Ko Te Riku, with their backs to the ocean, as per tradition.

Ahu Vai Uri

To orientate, this is the largest ahu and has five *moai* standing atop, in varying states of ruin. Interestingly, the individual *moai* represent different carving styles, as can be seen in their shape and surface textures. A sixth *moai* that should be on the left-hand side, can be found face-down a few metres away.

Ahu Tahai

Found off to the right of Ahu Vai Uri, this *ahu* contains a solitary *moai* that has eroded somewhat. The *ahu* itself was constructed around 700 CE, one of the oldest on Easter Island.

Ahu Ko Te Riku

The Northern-most *ahu* in the area, this fully restored platform has one 5.1m *moai* complete with *pukao* (top knot) and original coloured eyes. It is the only *moai* to have eyes, which were originally made of white coral.

Photo opportunities

- **Sunrise** - The good news is that you're likely to have the place to yourself, or maybe a few stray horses that have wandered by. Incorporating the sea into your photos adds to the story of the *moai* turning away from the sea and facing inland.

- **Sunset** - Expect to be in good company, as many people bring a picnic to watch the sun go down. Make sure you take your tripod, a telephoto lens, and look for an elevated position to capture people-free images of the *moai*.

200mm, f/3.5, ISO 1600, 1/250 sec
CF 1.5x camera

1.14 The fully restored Ahu Ko Te Riku enjoying the very last of the day's sun.

- **Explore the area** - The Ahu Tahai area was once a large settlement, although the stone buildings and ruins may go unnoticed, such is the hypnotic power of the *moai*. In addition, take a little time to check out the nearby cemetery (page 27).

105mm, f/11, ISO 200, 95 sec
FF camera

1.15 A long-exposure shot using a ND filter creates a sense of the *moai* standing still in time.

Ahu Tongariki

 #ahutongariki, #ahutongariki2

The site of the largest *ahu* on Easter Island, Ahu Tongariki is the centre for the Hotu Iti people of Rapa Nui. There are now 15 *moai* proudly standing with their backs to the sea. Unfortunately, the site has been subject to many civil wars and natural disasters that have damaged the *moai* over time.

After a devastating tsunami in the 1960s, a subsequent restoration effort was undertaken in the1990s to restore the site. However, only one of the *moai* is still sporting a *pukao* (top knot). More of the *pukao* are stacked neatly off to one side near the car park.

45mm, f/11, ISO 50, 1/15 sec FF camera

1.16 Cloud cover over Ahu Tongariki is common, however it can create dramatic images.

50mm, f/11, ISO 160, 1/250 sec FF camera

1.17 A *moai* lying face up at Ahu Tongariki, looking similar to the mountain in the background.

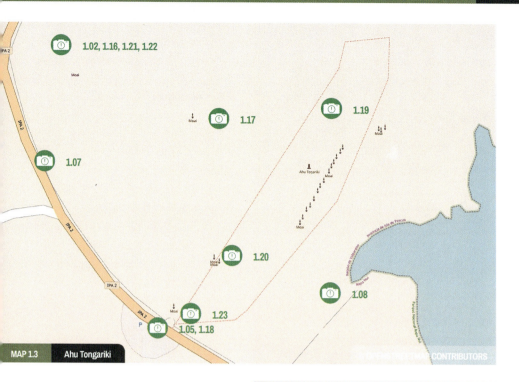

MAP 1.3 **Ahu Tongariki**

© OPENSTREETMAP CONTRIBUTORS

Photo tips and tricks

- **Sunrise** - Hands down, Ahu Tongariki is the place to be to watch the sun rise over Easter Island. Even if you choose to use a bike or other mode of transport to get around during the day, having a car to arrive for sunrise will make a lot of difference. Note that the official entry to the site starts at 09:00 / 09:30, although the entry post is manned at sunrise as well. Don't forget your Park access.

- **Close-up shots** - To get a photo of a starburst coming in from behind a *moai*, get up close to the giant *ahu* so that you are underneath the statues.

- **Along the perimeter** - There is a stone wall that surrounds Ahu Tongariki, which is an excellent stand-in for a tripod if you forgot yours. In addition, if you use a telephoto lens from this distance, you

120mm, f/8, ISO 200, 1/400 sec
CF 1.5x camera

1.18 The view from the carpark of the massive *ahu* of Ahu Tongariki.

50mm, f/16, ISO 400, 1/250 sec
FF camera

1.19 Dispelling the myth that the *moai* are just heads, the full bodies can be inspected.

24mm, f/16, ISO 400, 1/250 sec
FF camera

1.20 The red scoria *pukao* top knots lined up neatly at Ahu Tongariki.

can capture pleasing shots of the entire *ahu* with the *moai* all standing relatively close to each other (thanks to the compression that distance provides).

- **Summer solstice** - The people of Rapa Nui were keen astrological observers, and many *ahu* have been strategically positioned to align with the solstices. On the Summer solstice, all of the *moai* will face the sunset.

- **View from Rano Raraku** (page 30) - Keep an eye out for Ahu Tongariki when you are exploring nearby Rano Raraku. If you carry a telephoto lens, you will be able to get pleasing landscape photos of the Ahu Tongariki standing majestically near the sea.

 100mm, f/11, ISO 50, 1/15 sec
FF camera
1.21 The *moai* in dark shadows at Ahu Tongariki.

 200mm, f/4, ISO 250, 1/500 sec
CF 1.5x camera
1.22 Amazing pinks and purples during an overcast sunrise at Ahu Tongariki.

 55mm, f/11, ISO 125, 1/250 sec
FF camera
1.23 The full body of a solitary *moai* near the carpark at Ahu Tongariki.

Anakena

1.24 — 100mm, f/8, ISO 320, 1/200 sec
FF camera

Ahu Nau Nau, with Ahu Ature Huki peeking through the background at Anakena.

#anakena, #anakenabeach, #anakenabeach🏖️🌴

Anakena is one of the only two small beaches in Easter Island. The sandy beach is believed to be the landing place of Hotu Matu'a, the first ruler of Rapa Nui. It is also where the powerful chiefs of the Miru clan, the leading tribe of the island, established their residence. The area has two ahu, Ahu Ature Huki and Ahu Nau Nau.

Ahu Nau Nau

Ahu Nau Nau has one of the most elaborate and well-preserved *ahu* on Easter Island. Four of the seven *moai* still retain their red scoria *pukao*.

Ahu Ature Huki

Ahu Ature Huki is a lone *moai* that was restored by a Norwegian explorer in the 1950s with the help of locals using traditional statue erection techniques.

1.25 — 24mm, ISO 100, f/11, 1/200 sec
FF camera

The beach at Anakena, with the *moai* (centre and right) with their backs to the sea.

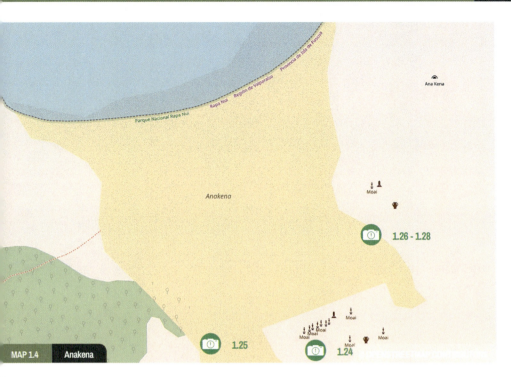

MAP 1.4   Anakena

1.26 - 1.28

1.25

1.24

Ana Kena

Moai

Anakena

Parque Nacional Rapa Nui   Rapa Nui   Región de Valparaíso   Provincia de Isla de Pascua

150mm, f/8, ISO 200, 1/400 sec
CF 1.5x camera

1.26   Top knots still intact on Ahu Nau Nau.

105mm, f/11, ISO 250, 1/250 sec
FF camera

1.27 Anakena is original landing site on Easter Island, with Ahu Nau Nau marking the spot.

Photo tips and tricks

- **Afternoon views** - The best light for Anakena and the *ahu / moai* is going to be in the afternoon, with the sun coming in from the West to illuminate the faces of the *moai*.

- **The beach** - This area is significant in the history of the Rapa Nui people, as it is believed to be the arrival place of the first settlers. Venture off to the left of the main *ahu* and use a wide-angle lens to capture both the beach and the statues all together.

150mm, f/8, ISO 200, 1/400 sec
CF 1.5x camera

1.28 The lone *moai* at Ahu Ature Huki was restored in the 1950s using traditional techniques.

1.29

30mm, f/11, ISO 160, 1/250 sec
FF camera

The low-rise buildings of the Orongo
ceremonial village shield from the high winds.

Orongo ceremonial village

#orongo, #orongovillage, #tangatamanu,
#ranokau, #ranokau2, #volcanranokau,
#ranokauvolcano, #ranokaucrater

Situated on the South Western edge of Easter Island,
Orongo ceremonial village is probably the most
dramatically situated location on the whole island. The
village sits on the cliff face looking out to the *motu* (small
islands) to the South West.

Ceremonial village

The stone village was considered sacred by the Rapa
Nui people to honour their god, Makemake. The village
features 53 low-rise buildings (i.e. not quite standing

1.30

105mm, f/11, ISO 320, 1/250 sec
FF camera

The islands off the coast of Orongo village
where key to the Tangata Manu ceremony.

 11mm, f/11, ISO 100, 1/800 sec
CF 1.5x camera

1.31   The lagoon-covered crater of Rano Kau.

room) that do a reasonable job of shielding people from the elements. The most famous of these buildings housed the only known basalt *moai*, Hoa Hakananai'a. It was taken in 1868 by the British Navy and now resides in the British Museum.

24mm, f/16, ISO 1000, 1/250 sec
FF camera

1.32   The small structures at Orongo ceremonial village with the small *motu* in the distance.

The buildings were oriented towards the *motu*, which were key to traditional ceremonies. The annual race, known as Tangata Manu, required participants to swim across to nearby Motu Nui to collect the first sooty tern (small bird) egg of the season. Many participants died from falling off the cliff faces or were eaten by sharks in the waters between the islands! All who took part in the ceremony lived in the specially constructed houses that line the crater. There are paintings that depict the ceremony inside some of these houses.

Rano Kau

With a height of 324 metres, Rano Kau is the largest volcano on Easter Island. The word "rano" in the Rapa Nui language refers to a volcano where water is stored. Venturing up to the Orongo village affords stunning views over the lagoon-covered crater, and the island in the distance.

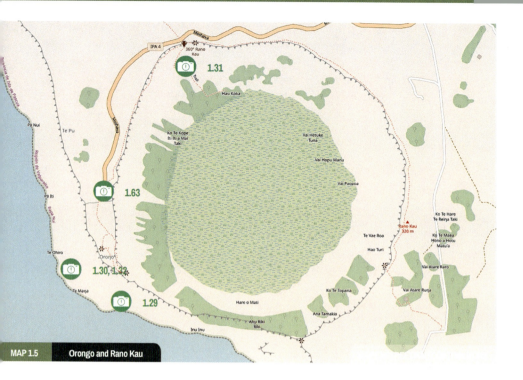

MAP 1.5 Orongo and Rano Kau

Photo tips and tricks

- **Single entry** - Unfortunately the access pass to Rapa Nui National Park only includes a single entry to the Orongo ceremonial village. However, you are able to visit Rano Kau at your leisure during opening hours.

- **There will be wind** - Both Rano Kau and the Orongo ceremonial village are quite exposed, meaning that it's going to be quite windy a lot of the time. This makes taking long exposure photos more difficult, unless you brace your camera (and tripod). Try lowering your stance and / or add weight to the tripod to improve stability.

- **Afternoon delight** - Where possible, plan your visit to the village for late afternoon (closing time is 18:00). This gives you the best chance of capturing the late afternoon glow coming in from the West. If you have the luxury of time, leave your decision as to when to visit Orongo until the last minute, holding out for optimal light (as you only get one visit).

- **Hiking up to Rano Kau** - There is a 4km path that starts from the base of Rano Kau at the edge of Hanga Roa. Look for signs for Te Ara O Te Ao, and the path should take around 1.5 to 2 hours to reach the Orongo ceremonial village.

Rano Raraku

105mm, f/11, ISO 160, 1/250 sec
FF camera

1.33 The unfinished and abandoned *moai* at Rano Raraku has a surreal look.

> # #ranoraraku, #ranoraraku🗿, #ranorarakuquarry, #ranorarakumoai

Rano Raraku is the volcanic crater that produced the majority of the materials used to create the *moai*. In fact, this stone quarry is still littered with *moai* of different shapes and sizes, most are unfinished / abandoned. This includes the largest *moai* found, at 21.6m, and estimated to weigh a whopping 270 tonnes.

Keep an eye out for Tukuturi, a distinct *moai* that looks like a bearded man in a kneeling position. It represents a pose that islanders form when performing choruses in *riu* (festivals).

The crater is also one of the sources of freshwater for the islanders. Animals can be seen grazing here, and visitor may not be permitted to wander about freely.

40mm, f/11, ISO 500, 1/250 sec
FF camera

1.34 The excavation of *moai* from the rock is clearly visible at Rano Raraku.

 70mm, f/8, ISO 200, 1/500 sec
CF 1.5x camera

1.35 More *moai* than humans at Rano Raraku, the rock quarry of Easter Island.

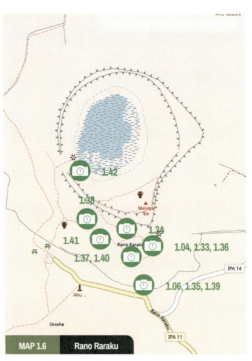

1.42

1.38

Ma'unga
Eo

1.41

1.34

Rano Raraku

1.04, 1.33, 1.36

1.37, 1.40

IPA 14

1.06, 1.35, 1.39

Ahu ...

Oroihe

IPA 11

MAP 1.6 | **Rano Raraku**

 24mm, f/11, ISO 200, 1/250 sec
FF camera

1.36 Tukuturi, a representation of a pose islanders adopt when performing *rui*.

 80mm, f/11, ISO 200, 1/250 sec
FF camera

1.37 The *moai* at Rano Raraku were abandoned for various reasons, or not finished.

Photo tips and tricks

- **Single entry** - Unfortunately the access pass to Rapa Nui National Park only includes a single entry to the Rano Raraku volcano area.

- **Dodging the shadows** - The best times to visit are around opening and closing times, where the shadows caused by the sun are minimal. A cloudy day can become a blessing in disguise, with the sun acting as a giant soft box. This creates much more even light, lessening the harshness of shadows under the *moai*.

- **Don't forget the crater** - The prolific sprinkling of *moai* as you approach the site can be a little hypnotic. You'll need to walk back towards the main entrance and follow a separate path to get to the crater. This path isn't so well maintained and can feel as though you're walking through a field at

times. Once you have arrived, keep an eye out for the horses and other animals that come to drink at the crater.

40mm, f/11, ISO 200, 1/250 sec
FF camera
1.38   One of many "head and shoulders" *moai*.

70mm, f/8, ISO 200, 1/500 sec
CF 1.5x camera
1.39   The rock quarry of Rano Raraku includes the largest *moai*, at 21.6m and 270 tonnes.

100mm, f/11, ISO 500, 1/250 sec
FF camera

1.40 Details on the *moai* include tattoos and distinct facial features.

 80mm, f/11, ISO 500, 1/250 sec
FF camera

1.41 The ground swallowing up the *moai*.

 105mm, f/11, ISO 200, 1/250 sec
FF camera

1.42 The often missed / ignored crater at Rano Raraku including a number of unused *moai*.

 24mm, f/11, ISO 400, 1/250 sec
FF camera

1.43   What appears to be a cave is actually evidence of a small village at Ahu Akahanga.

Caves

Introduction

Something that not many people are aware of is that the tiny Easter Island has a large *ana* (cave) system. The caves have been largely formed by volcanic lava, creating relatively smooth tubular designs. However, many caves are in reality tiny carve-outs in a cliff that are sometimes large enough for one person to shelter.

The native population documented their exploration of over 800 caves. These caves often served as refuge from the elements as well as during times of war amongst the clans. Most families had their "own" caves, where valuables could be stored, ceremonies conducted, and even the birth of new additions to the clan.

Ana Kai Tangata

> **#**   #anakaitangata, #anakaitangatacave

Ana Kai Tangata is often nicknamed the "cave of cannibals" because the meaning of its name in the Rapa Nui language has been interpreted to mean "cave where men are eaten", although archaeological evidence hasn't (yet) supported this claim. Despite the eeriness of its name, Ana Kai Tangata is one of the most interesting and accessible caves on Easter Island, nearby to Hanga Roa. Its walls feature beautiful paintings depicting the *manutara* (sooty tern bird) that migrate and nest every Spring on the island.

Ana Hue Neru

#anaokeke

Located on the remote Northern side of Poike in the North of the island, the two caves Ana O Keke (for young women) and Ana More Matu Puku (for young men) played a role in the ritual of Ana Ana Hue Neru. The *neru* ritual involved the whitening of selected young women and men through seclusion in caves. They were kept in the caves until they have fairer complexion, with food being brought to them by family members. There are petroglyphs in the Ana O Keke cave that depict the ritual, although the authenticity of these petroglyphs has been called into question in recent times.

Note that accessing these caves is a bit of an undertaking, so you may want to enlist the help of a local guide.

Ana Kakenga

#anakakenga, anakakengacave

Ana Kakenga is an approximately 50m volcanic tube cave on the East of the island. It often became a place of refuge during the clan wars that regularly took place.

The entrance of the cave is a small hole at ground level, difficult to spot without the aid of a local guide, and not suitable to those who suffer from claustrophobia. The cave descends and leads to two large natural windows that are 30 metres high, providing atmospheric views of the ocean.

Ana Te Pahu

#anatepahu, #bananacave

Located on the foothill of the Ma'unga Terevaka volcano (page 40), Ana Te Pahu is the largest cave system on Easter Island at approximately 7km in length. The name Ana Te Pahu translates as "cave of the drum", due to the hardened lava that creates a drum effect when struck. Archaeologists believe that the cave was used by the first inhabitants as a dwelling place. This is evidenced by the existence of *manavai* (enclosed garden beds) and *umu pae* (old stone ovens).

Note that due to risk of collapse, it may not be possible to access much of the cave.

Ana Te Pora

#anatepora

Ana Te Pora ("Cave of the reed canoe") is located on the East coast of the island near Ana Kakenga (page 35) and Ahu Akivi (page 16). Ana Te Pora links through a cave system to Ana Te Pahu as well.

The interior isn't so large however you can observe a large stone structure that resembles either a giant bed or a burial plot. It is presumed to be the latter, or a ceremonial altar, as the locals typically slept on the ground.

24mm, f/11, ISO 160, 1/250 sec
FF camera

1.44   A solitary *pukao* (top knot) sits in the distance of the main *ahu* at Ahu Vinapu (top left).

Exploring the park

The sites on Easter Island are accessible by road, with the exception of many of the cave systems (page 34). There is a main arterial road that crosses through the interior of the island, linking Hanga Roa (page 44) with Anakena (page 24). There is a long coastal road that makes its way along the South East of the island back to Hanga Roa, providing easy access to many of the key sites.

Once you've made your way through the top sites (page 15), make sure that you allow sufficient time to spend at the places below. Not only do they have more *moai* to photograph, some of the archaeological sites help provide more detail about how the Rapa Nui people lived.

Ahu Akahanga

#	#ahuakahanga

Found to the East of Hanga Roa, Ahu Akahanga isn't as well preserved as most other *ahu* sites across the island. Don't let its current state deceive you, as Ahu Akahanga was one of the more important historical sites for Easter Island. It is also the burial place of Hotu Matu'a (the first chief of Easter Island). Here you can see the remains of a small village, as well as the unrestored 18m *ahu* and 13 *moai*. In addition, you can see up-close several *pukao* that are dotted around the site.

40mm, f/11, ISO 250, 1/250 sec
FF camera

1.45 A *moai* that has toppled off a ruined *ahu* at Ahu Akahanga.

 55mm, f/11, ISO 250, 1/250 sec
FF camera

1.46 Remains of several *pukao* at Ahu Akahanga.

1.43 1.46
1.45
1.47

© OPENSTREETMAP CONTRIBUTORS

MAP 1.7   Ahu Akahanga

 35mm, f/16, ISO 320, 1/250 sec
FF camera

1.47 The ruined *pukao* and *moai* at Ahu Akahanga.

1.48 35mm, f/11, ISO 125, 1/250 sec
FF camera
The interlocked masonry at Ahu Vinapu looks suspiciously like the work of the Incans.

Ahu Vinapu

#ahuvinapu

Ahu Vinapu is a neatly maintained site at the Eastern edge of the Hanga Roa airport. It is the archaeological site of one of the largest *ahu*, oriented to face the sunrise during the Winter solstice. The stonemasonry consists of large, carefully fitted slabs of basalt, reminiscent of the Incan designs seen in Cusco (Peru).

1.49 35mm, f/11, ISO 320, 1/250 sec
FF camera
The damaged head of a *moai* at Ahu Vinapu.

1.50 105mm, f/11, ISO 200, 1/250 sec
FF camera
The scale of the *ahu* at Ahu Vinapu is best viewed from a distance.

Ahu Te Peu

#ahutepeu

Ahu Te Peu is a large *ahu* site on the North East side of Easter Island. The site has not been restored, and so provides a glimpse into the state of ruins since the Rapa Nui native inhabitants left. It has fallen *moai* and evidence of a large stone village. In addition, you can see stone *manavai* (walled gardens, to shield plants from the elements), and the foundations of *hare paenga* (boat houses), named because of their elliptical shape.

100mm, f/11, ISO 250, 1/250 sec
FF camera

1.51 The toppled *moai* visible in the distance at Ahu Te Pito Kura.

Ahu Te Pito Kura

#ahutepitokura

Located on the North coast in front of the Bay of La Perouse, Te Pito Kura is the site of the largest *moai* statue ever mounted on an *ahu*. The *moai* is named Paro, weighs approximately 80 tonnes, and its *pukao* (12 tonnes) is one of the largest carved. The *moai* now lies face down on the ground with its body split in half.

Also on the site is a large oval-shaped stone 80cm in diameter, believed to contain special qualities. This may be due to the stone's high iron content which causes the it to retain heat differently to nearby rocks, and also to interfere with magnetic compasses. The expression "Te Pito Kura" means "navel of light", which is believed to be attributed to this stone (it's quite round and smooth).

100mm, f/11, ISO 160, 1/250 sec
FF camera

1.52 A toppled *moai* and *pukao* combo off the *ahu* at Ahu Te Pito Kura.

Poike

#poike

Poike is one of the three volcanoes on Easter Island, and occupies a sizeable chunk of real estate on the North East of the island. The volcano is approximately 400 metres high, and nearby is a series of *moai* lying face down on the ground and the Ana o Keke cave (page 35).

Ma'unga Terevaka

#maungaterevaka, #terevaka

With a height of 507 metres above sea level, Ma'unga Terevaka is both the youngest and tallest volcano on Easter Island. The 1.5 hours trek to the top affords you panoramic views across the island, and really instills the feeling of how remote the island is.

Papa Vaka sea petroglyphs

#papavaka

This archaeological site is on the North of the island and lies between Pu o Hiro and Ahu Te Pito Kura (page 39). The petroglyphs are carved on the large slabs of basalt rock. They depict maritime motifs such as *vaka* (canoe), *mangai* (fishhook), *heke* (octopus), and *pikea* (crabs).

The feature petroglyph is a rendition of a *vaka* (canoe) with two 12m hulls and is the largest petroglyph on the island. There is also the papa *mangai* (rock of hooks) with is largest display of *mangai* figures on the island. The *mangai* was used to catch the important *kahi* (tuna).

24mm, f/11, ISO 1250, 1/250 sec
FF camera
1.53   The petroglyph known as Papa Mangai - look for the fish hooks.

Puna Pau

#punapau

Both an extinct volcano and the quarry of red scoria, Puna Pau was an important site for the creation of the *pukao* (top knot) that adorned each *moai*. Found on the outskirts of Hanga Roa, Puna Pau today is a grassy outcrop with around 25 red scoria *pukao* jutting out of its Southern slope. Puna Pau is a little bit hidden from the rest of the island, although the site is accessible by road.

24mm, f/11, ISO 320, 1/250 sec
FF camera
1.54   What look like tyre tracks are actually depictions of two 12m hulls on Papa Vaka.

Capturing life on Easter Island

The original Polynesian inhabitants and their culture have been subject to erosion and phasing out by waves of settlers over the centuries. As a consequence, lifestyles have adapted to that of colonisers. Today, much of Easter Island's population is dedicated to the tourism industry, the island's big cash cow.

For those in search of insight into the past, Rapa Nui National Park (page 11) is your natural starting place. To explore traditions of the people, check out Museo Rapa Nui (page 46) and book a spot to watch some traditional dancing (page 48), even if you sense that many are shows put on for tourists. If possible, consider timing your trip to watch (or even participate) in one of the annual festivals (page 51).

30mm, f/11, ISO 1600, 1/100 sec FF camera

1.55 Horses out for a morning stroll near Ahu Tahai.

Hanga Roa

#hangaroa, #hangaroa

Hanga Roa is the only city on Easter Island. Originally used as the site to contain the locals of Rapa Nui when Chile annexed the island in 1888. At that time, the locals were not allowed to leave the area and venture out, as the rest of the island became pastures for sheep that roamed freely. Fortunately, things eventually changed, and the locals were granted rights again after the 1964 uprising led by Alfonso Rapu.

Today, Hanga Roa is divided into two major hubs – Atamu Tekena Street and Te Pito or Te Henua treet. Atamu Tekena starts from Hotu Matu'a Avenue and ends at the airport. It is where you can find the Rapa Nui Parliament, the Chilean Navy, pharmacy, as well as many shops, hotels, restaurants, offices, and supermarkets.

1.56 24mm, f/11, ISO 400, 1/250 sec
FF camera
The vibrant colours of the Easter Island cemetery, mixing Rapa Nui and Catholicism.

Te Pito Street also has a number of shops, restaurants, hotels, and other commercial buildings. It starts at the edge of the sea at Hanga Roa Otai (page 44) and ends at the Church of Santa Cruz (below).

1.57 35mm, f/11, ISO 250, 1/250 sec
FF camera
Fishing boats moored in the morning at Hanga Roa Otai.

90mm, f/11, ISO 400, 1/250 sec
FF camera

1.58 An incredibly well restored (or fake) *moai* in Hanga Roa.

© OPENSTREETMAP CONTRIBUTORS

MAP 2.1   Hanga Roa

	A	Ahu Huri a Urenga		E	Hanga Kio'e
	B	Ahu Tahai		F	Hanga Piko
	C	Museo Rapa Nui		G	Hanga Roa Otai
	D	Easter Island cemetery		H	Parroquia De La Santa Cruz

Most people aren't going to spend much time in Hanga Roa, however there's definitely an island charm that makes it worth exploring a little. Below are the main places to check out:

Parroquia de la Santa Cruz

The Parroquia de la Santa Cruz ("Parish of the Holy Cross") is the Catholic church for Easter Island. Established in 1937, the church contains many nods to religious icons of Easter Island, blending them in with traditional Catholic motifs.

Logistics

Tickets and opening times

 Monday to Friday: 09:00 - 13:00 and 16:00 - 19:00.

🎟 *Free*

Hanga Piko

> \#   #hangapiko, #ahuriata

The Hanga Piko ("Hidden bay") is a small man-made port for local fishermen. Its name stems from being in a semi-tucked away location. Here, the locals try to maintain traditional fishing for different species of fish including barracuda, kana-kana, tuna, and albacore. You can also observe sea turtles if you are patient.

Ahu Riata

Ahu Riata is an ahu that was restored in 1998. The *ahu* supports a lone *moai* with a rather unforgiving expression on its face.

Ahu Huri a Urenga

> \#   #ahuhuriaurenga

Similar to Ahu Akivi (page 16), this *ahu* is one of the 25 platforms not found by the coastal areas. Of note is the fact that the sole *moai* has two pairs of hands, for reasons still not quite understood. A nearby well has been discovered to have been designed to determine seasons through observing the reflections of the light from the water. This has added astrological significance to the site.

Note that this *ahu* resides on private property, and is not part of the National Park.

Easter Island cemetery

Worth a stop on your way from Hanga Roa to Ahu Tahai. The cemetery contains many tombstones that are covered with both Christian and traditional Rapa Nui influences.

Museo Rapa Nui

> \#   #museorapanui
>
>   http://museorapanui.gob.cl/sitio (in Spanish)

Opened in 1973, the museum is also named after the pioneering Franciscan priest Sebastian Englert who spent his last 30 years from 1935 cataloguing much of the history of Easter Island. The museum houses the only female moai on the island as well as several traditional wood statuettes, photos, and archives of traditional music.

Logistics

Tickets and opening times

🕐 Tuesday to Friday: 09:30 - 17:30.
Saturday and Sunday: 09:30 - 12:30.
Monday: closed

🎫 *Free*

 24mm, f/11, ISO 400, 1/250 sec
FF camera

1.59 The fishing port of Hanga Roa Otai with one of the Ahu Tautira *moai* visible on the left.

Daily life

The traditional Easter Island diet is based primarily on seafood including fish, lobsters, and shrimp. Visitors from the mainland brought with them many South American staples over the centuries, including taro, sweet potato, plantain, yam, and sugar cane. There is ongoing debate as to when, and how, certain South American vegetables reached Easter Island, including suggestion of links to the ancient Incans.

Eating

Traditional food is usually simple and often wrapped in banana leaves and roasted in a *umu pae* (traditional earth oven). Just like ovens elsewhere in the world, the *umu pae* is also used by the locals for baking.

Here are some local dishes that you should try.

Po'e

Po'e is Easter Island's version of the sponge cake dessert. It is made from plantain, pumpkin, and arrowroot flour, and baked in an *umu pae*.

Tunu Ahi

Freshly caught fish which is then cleaned and sliced immediately and cooked on hot stones or *umu pae*.

Umu / Rapa Nui Curanto

The most common and traditional dish of Rapa Nui, *umu rapa nui* consists of meat, chicken, fish, and root crops. Preparation starts by wrapping all the ingredients together in banana leaves and cooking it in a hole in the ground covered with hot stones. The cooking time is slow and long thus making the *umu rapa nui* a community dish.

Traditional dancing and music

The traditional dances and music on Easter Island are of Polynesian origins. Traditional dances are often accompanied by ancestral instruments like the *hio* (bamboo flute), *upa-upa* (an accordion), and *kauaha* (a horse jaw that produces characteristic sounds when hit against the ground). There are options in Hanga Roa to watch a traditional dance performance, which are often put on for tourists. Enquire at your hotel for more information.

 24mm, f/11, ISO 125, 1/400 sec
FF camera

1.60 Looking out East towards Poike, one of the three volcanoes on Easter Island.

 80mm, f/11, ISO 800, 1/250 sec
FF camera

1.61 A *moai* showing off design motifs, propped up on an *artificial* ahu outside Hanga Roa.

Logistics

Planning your trip

When to visit

Travelling to Easter Island feels like a "once in a lifetime" trip because of its remoteness and cost. The island offers unforgettable moments no matter when you visit. However, summer months from December to March, are the best weather, with January and February being the peak tourist season. This includes cruise ships that tend to make regular stop-offs during the peak months. We could say "if you want to avoid the crowd, go at this time...", however crowds aren't exactly an issue on Easter Island.

A sub-tropical climate, average annual temperature is around 20°C (68°F), with around a 7°C (15°F) variance through the year. It's worth noting that the low season is from April to November, a large chunk of the year. In particular, the rainy season occurs during April and May. This means that prices will be lower, including flights.

Expected weather conditions

- **Summer** - December through to March is the summer season on Easter Island, with relatively high humidity levels.

- **Peak season** - January and February is the peak season and also the warmest. The temperature can usually reach up to 27°C (80°C), however made pleasant by the sea breeze.

- **Rainy season** - Nominally called so, although it is hardly tropical storms. The wettest months are April and May, followed by July and August.

- **Low season** - Stretching all the way from April through to November, average temperatures are still pleasant during the day. At night, a jacket will be necessary.

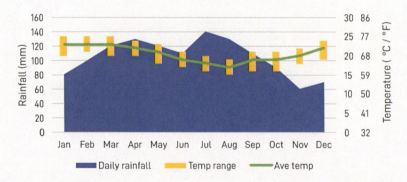

Weather conditions including the daily temperature range, and average rainfall each month.

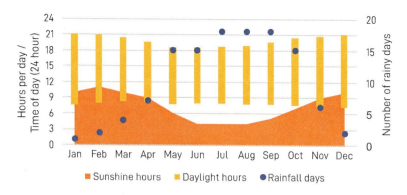

Expected light conditions by month, including daylight hours, average hours of sunshine each day. The number of rainfall days indicates the likelihood of overcast or cloudy days.

Light conditions

The graph below illustrates the expected light conditions throughout the year on Easter Island. Key points to note:

- **Sunshine hours** - The chances of a "nice" day.

- **Daylight hours** - The yellow bar graph indicates sunrise, sunset, and how many hours of daylight. Longer days in the Summer.

- **Rainfall days** - Indicates the likelihood of overcast or cloudy days, as well as rain.

Festive and holiday calendar

The holiday calendar of Easter Island largely reflects the Catholic influences brought by Chilean explorers. A few traditional festivals are slowly gaining prominence too.

January

1	New Year's Day

February

varies	Tapati Rapa Nui (Rapa Nui week)

April

varies	Easter Friday (the Friday after Good Friday)

May

1	Labour Day
21	Battle of Iquique Day
varies	Corpus Christi (held 60 days after Easter Sunday)

June

21	Winter solstice (great for photography options)
29	Saints Peter and Paul Day

August

15	Assumption Day

September

19	Glories of the Army Day

October

12	Columbus Day

November

1	All Saints' Day

December

8	Conception Day
21	Summer solstice (great for photography options)
25	Christmas Day

Booking in advance

Like most places that require a bit of time and effort to get to, the earlier that you book the better. This is particularly important for securing flights and

Tip

Flights to Easter Island are very much a seller's market, with LATAM Airways the only provider. However, keep an eye on flight costs for both Economy and Business Class (it's a full-service cabin). Sometimes the Business Class flight can actually be cheaper than Economy, depending on demand.

In any case, book your flights as early as possible.

accommodation. If you are heading to Easter Island during peak season, consider also signing up for the tourist staples such as a traditional dance. Note that the dancing display may conflict with sunset, and photographers tend to favour the latter!

Advanced tip

Due to high winds, medical emergencies, and other random factors, there's a chance that your flight going to / from Easter Island can be delayed or cancelled. Have a backup plan that includes at least a day of wiggle room, particularly on the Santiago de Chile side.

At the end of the day, getting stuck on Easter Island for an extra day is hardly the worst thing that can happen.

How to get to Easter Island

Most visitors get to Easter Island by air, and it's the most feasible option. Cruises and other boats do stop by however flying is by far the most sensible approach.

Air

Mataveri Internal Airport, or Isla de Pascua Airport (IATA code: IPC) has daily flights from Santiago de Chile with LATAM Airways. Flight time is around 4.5 hours. It is a domestic flight within Chile, and so there is no border control or immigration coming in from Santiago de Chile.

The LATAM Airways flights often go on to Papeete (Tahiti), and so you may encounter passengers that are transiting through Easter Island.

Note that the planes are the primary means of evacuating islanders if there's a medical emergency. On occasion, a passenger could be bumped in preference to somebody who needs to get to a hospital on the mainland. Fortunately, this doesn't occur too often.

Tip
Make sure you get a window seat on the left side of the plane for best views taking off and landing. Keep your camera handy.

Tour company / hotel transfer

If you have booked a tour package for Easter Island, chances are that your tour company will greet you at the airport. If not, reach out to your hotel in case they offer a collection service. This is particularly helpful if you arrive at night.

Taxi

If you are feeling particularly intrepid, you could walk from the airport into town. However, taxis are cheap and a trip costs around CLP 3,000.

Boat

It is possible to reach Easter Island by boat and for that, you have three options, in order of feasibility.

Cruise ship

There are cruise options that berth near Easter Island, although the swells make it more challenging for most destinations. These cruises typically stay for a couple of days, which is often enough time to capture the highlights.

Chilean Navy

The Chilean Navy travels to Easter Island twice a year from Valparaiso on the mainland. Seats for civilians are limited, and you'll need to be comfortable with being at sea for a period of time, with luxury not being the highest priority.

Private yacht

If you have chartered (or own) a private yacht to take you to Easter Island (or just to sail the South Pacific seas), you will need an experienced pilot to manoeuvre the boat to near the shore. You can anchor at either Hanga Roa bay (page 44) or Anakena beach (page 24).

Accommodation

Despite being one of the remotest places on earth, Easter Island has varied options for accommodations to fit your budget and preferences. However, don't expect large sprawling hotel chains. Hotels have been built to integrate with the natural surroundings where possible, as part of local efforts to retain the traditional aesthetic of the island.

Typically, you can expect to pay double the price of a similar accommodation option on the mainland. Here are the most common accommodation options to consider.

Hotels

Hotels on Easter Island are in or close to Hanga Roa. Mid-range hotels usually cost around $100 to $150 per night whilst high-end rooms cost from $300 to $500 a night.

Cabins

Cabin or *cabaña* rentals have grown in popularity in recent years. The size of these cabins can fit two people or even a family. One advantage of this type of accommodation is that it has a kitchen which allows you to prepare your own meals.

Budget private rooms

Private budget accommodation is a cheaper alternative to hotels. They will give you access to a private bathroom and a few amenities. However, you are more likely to find these accommodation options on the outskirts of Hanga Roa.

Camping

Camping is the cheapest option for those who are on a budget. Easter Island has a few campsites that overlook the ocean, with basic facilities. Rates usually start at $13 per person per night.

Electricity

Hanga Roa has electricity all day although since the main source of power comes from a series of diesel generators, there are occasional blackouts. Easter Island (and all of Chile) supplies 220-230 Volts ("240V" as marked on electrical devices) and 50Hz. Wall sockets are mostly Type C (Euro two-pin) and Type L (Italian three pin, with the middle pin being a ground pin).

Check your devices before plugging them in and turning the electricity on. Most modern electronics can handle 110V-240V and 50-60Hz. For items such as hair dryers or anything with a motor or heating element in it, pay particular attention. Devices that are 110-120V won't work in 220-240V sockets.

Visas

Easter Island is part of Chile, so unless you are arriving from Papeete (Tahiti), you should already have a Chilean visa before heading to Easter Island.

Chile allows 92 countries to stay without a visa for up to 90 days, including European Union, Americas, and many countries across Asia (including New Zealand). However, "reciprocity fees" are in place when flying into Chile via Santiago de Chile International Airport (no other entry point, including from Tahiti) for several countries. The prices are currently set at (end of 2019):

- United States passport holders - $US 131
- Canadian passport holders - $US 132
- Australian passport holders - $US 117
- Mexican passport holders - $US 23

40mm, f/11, ISO 100, 1/250 sec
FF camera
1.62   The many toppled *moai* at Ahu Vinapu.

Making the most of your time

Getting around

Because of its size, it shouldn't be a surprise that Easter Island has no real public transportation to speak of. At a pinch, locals are friendly and are willing to give you a ride to your destination in case you find yourself stranded or lost.

Below are your transport options. We have not mentioned horseback riding as this mode of transport is limited to tours.

Car hire

If you want to have complete control of your time, renting a car is the best option for exploring Easter Island. In order to get into position for sunrise and sunset locations across the island, this is by far the most sensible option.

The car rental options on Easter Island are, shall we say, a little less formal than elsewhere. Quite often, you'll be essentially borrowing somebody's car for the day, at a price. This means that you are unlikely to have much of a choice of car options. This includes only having access to manual transmission cars, unless you want to pay a hefty premium.

Owing to the limited options, we offer a word of caution here on insurance – there really isn't any! You will have to cover damages incurred to the vehicle while you're using it, as insurance isn't going to be part of the arrangement.

You should also be careful when driving after dark in rural areas as cows and horses often roam about. Horses often won't move and expect you to give way to them. A stand-off between a belligerent horse and car is both hilarious and frustrating, in equal measure.

Taxi

There is a good taxi service on the island with which you can arrange an itinerary, for a price. However, this does require coordination of pickup times, which may affect your ability to get a good shot. Note that mobile phone reception can be inconsistent as well and shouldn't be relied on to call a taxi.

Bicycle hire

There are several businesses in town that rent bicycles. The main road to Anakena is paved, however venturing further often involves unpaved roads. In addition, this may not be the most convenient form of transport if you want to get to places such as Ahu Tongariki (page 20) for sunrise.

50mm, f/11, ISO 400, 1/800 sec
FF camera

1.63 The aquatic motifs adorning a boulder outside the Orongo ceremonial village.

Tours / tour guides

The majority of Easter Island is accessible without the aid of a tour guide. Where they are necessary is if you want to start exploring the many caves. This is due to the challenge of finding the entrances for some, and the safety due to the chances of rock fall.

Advantages to tours

- You're supporting the local economy.
- You have a local who knows the ins and outs of the area and is typically knowledgeable about the places being visited.
- Someone can give you helpful tips and suggestions for your itinerary.
- The tour guide can help navigate language challenges and act as an impromptu translator (although this isn't likely to come up on Easter Island).

Potential downsides

- If you are on a budget, it might be expensive for you.
- You might experience information overload from all the facts presented to you by the guide.
- Depending on the tour, and the participants, you may have little to no control over the schedule. This can result in lots of waiting for others, and not being in a place at the optimum time of day for light (key to capturing great photos).

A compromise could be to take a tour as a "taster" and to give you some basic information to work with. You can then return at a later time when the light is better to get the images that you were after. This strategy works best if you have planned for a longer time on Easter Island.

Practicalities

Mobile phones and internet access

We'll set expectations up-front – mobile phone coverage on Easter Island isn't fantastic, and internet access is going to be quite slow. Don't expect to be able to use streaming services etc at great speeds here, particularly in the evenings.

SIM cards

The two main mobile phone providers that provide coverage on Easter Island are Entel and Movistar. Ideally, you have already obtained a SIM card on the mainland. If you are caught short, you can visit the Entel store (near Banco Estado) in Hanga Roa.

Take your passport with you to pick up a SIM card in case identification is required.

Tip

For the time and hassle, seriously consider using roaming services with your existing provider if they cover Chile. At the end of the day, the coverage on Easter Island is very bare bones, and useful mostly for emergencies / short calls and not data services.

WiFi access

Hotels invariably have WiFi access, however as noted earlier, speeds aren't going to be amazing. Many restaurants and bars offer free WiFi to patrons, although you may need to ask the wait staff for the password.

Money

Currency

The US dollar and the Chilean peso are the two currencies accepted on Easter Island. Larger ticket costs, such as car hire and accommodation, are invariably negotiated in US dollars. However, you might want to do the math and check which currency is better for you. Taxi drivers also accept US dollars as payment but keep smaller bills ready in hand as drivers tend not have change with them (a global phenomenon, apparently).

Where to exchange

Most hotels offer some currency conversion services for major currencies, although rates are typically very uncompetitive. The two banks on the island, Santander and Banco Estado, will offer better conversion rates however their opening hours can be limited (page 58).

Credit card / debit card acceptance

Many small vendors only accept cash, however most shops and restaurants take credit cards. Be careful, though, because most of them tack on a service fee for the privilege.

Tip

For more significant costs of your journey, mainly flights and accommodation, try to purchase these online in your home currency. This dramatically reduces the likelihood of cards being blocked as anti-fraud measures. Often the time taken to have a card unlocked can be frustrating, and potentially expensive if you have to make overseas calls.

Tipping

Tipping is often optional, however 10% may be added to restaurant bills.

Typical opening hours

The pace of life on Easter Island is much slower than the mainland, and so it is not surprising to discover that most stores do not open early. Opening times are typically around 09:30 or 10:00. Shops may close in the afternoon between 14:00 and 17:00 and resume until 22:00. Banks and other services either don't open for the afternoon, or close by 18:00. Some mini markets stay open until midnight.

Rapa Nui National Park access

An access pass to Rapa Nui National Park should be provided on arrival to all tourists, such is its importance to your trip to Easter Island. In any case, factor in purchase of a pass to your budget for the trip. The larger archaeological sites are manned by CONAF (Forestry Corporation) officers, and your access card will be inspected each time. In addition, you are expected to have an access card at any time that you are in the National Park (which is almost half of Easter Island).

Note that the access card only permits one single entry into Rano Raraku (page 30) and the Orongo ceremonial village (page 27).

Tickets are valid for 10 days.

Ticket office opening hours

CONAF office – Hanga Roa

- April to November: 09:00 to 18:00.
- December to March: 09:00 to 19:00.

Airport

The opening hours coincide with the arrival of flights. Look for the large signs before you get to baggage collection.

Tip
Purchase your tickets at the airport, it will save you a lot of time. In addition, it will give you something to do whilst your bags are unloaded from the plane.

Tickets can also be purchased at the Ma'u Henua office on Atamu Tekena street.

Prices

Prices accurate as of September 2019, however visit the CONAF website (www.conaf.cl/parques/parque-nacional-rapa-nui/, in Spanish) for further information.

Chilean nationals

- Adults - $US 20
- Children - $US 10

Foreigners

- Adults - $US 80
- Children - $US 40

Language

Rapa Nui is the native language of Easter Island (also known as Rapa Nui, as are the native population). It is a Polynesian language, sharing a lot of commonality with languages including Tahitian, Hawaiian, and Maori (New Zealand). Rapa Nui is an oral language, as written language documents (known as Rongorongo) have yet to be deciphered.

Sadly, centuries of occupation and dominance has eroded the speaking population of the language. Most younger generation islanders grow up speaking Spanish, the national language of Chile. Since tourism is the main source of income for the island, basic English is spoken by most people.

Glossary of terms

- **Ahu** - Shrine or place of worship, called marae in other parts of Polynesia
- **Hare moa** - Chicken coop
- **Hare paenga** - Boat house
- **Heke** - Octopus
- **Kahi** - Tuna
- **Makemake** - Rapa Nui fertility god, creator of humanity, and overseer of the tangata manu tradition.
- **Mana** - Supernatural powers
- **Manavai** - stone-enclosed garden bed
- **Mangai** - Fishhook
- **Manutara** - Sooty tern (bird native to the area)
- **Moai** - Statue (page 14)
- **Motu** - Small island
- **Pikea** - Crabs
- **Pukao** - Cylindrical stone topknots carved of red scoria and placed on the heads of *moai* (page 14)
- **Rapa Nui** - Easter Island, Easter Islanders, and their language
- **Tangata manu** - Literally "bird man", it is the name given to the festival (page 28)
- **Tiki** - Carved figures of the human form
- **Umu** - Earthen oven
- **Vaka** - canoe

Staying healthy

Drinking water

The tap water on Easter Island is alright to drink for most people, however it has a higher than normal salt and chlorine taste. If you have a sensitive stomach, it's better to be on the safe side and stick to bottled water.

Despite this, however, it is still wise to take the necessary precautions and use bottled water for drinking. It's better to be safe than sorry.

Food / drinks

Everything on Easter Island is expensive; it's a remote island. However, there is no specific reason to be concerned about the food or drink produce. Keep an eye out for the usual suspects that can cause food spoilage. Avoid anything that is not cooked and has been sitting about for a while after being peeled / cut (e.g. fruit). Also avoid eating raw vegetables, fresh salads, and raw shellfish.

When drinking, you should also be aware of crushed ice in your drink. Although manufactured ice uses purified water, the blocks of ice could get contaminated during transport.

A brief history of Easter Island

Located approximately 3,500 km off the West coast of Chile, Easter Island (Rapa Nui in Polynesian) is one of the remotest places on the planet. The name "Easter Island" (also *Isla de Pascua* in Spanish) stems from its discovery on Easter Sunday in 1772 by Dutch explorers. The unique *moai* have proven to be quite the drawcard that has helped sustain the island through tourism.

Rapa Nui was first settled by seafaring Polynesians coming from the West, sometime between the 5th and 12th century CE. This wide window for the potential settlement date is a testament to the impact that the native population would go on to have on the island. Legends describe the first immigrants being led by Hoto-Matua, the island's first king. The group travelled by canoe and landed up at Anakena.

Historians speculate that as the community grew, each tribe became more ambitious and decided to build gigantic *moai*, the evidence of which we can see today. There is archaeological evidence of the destruction of earlier *moai*, believed to be a combination of the outcome of wars, and to make way for larger statues. Archaeologists speculate that the islanders' obsession with *ahu* and *moai* construction had a deleterious effect on the island's limited resources, particularly the trees that were originally present.

After initial discovery by the Dutch, in 1770 the Spanish viceroy of Peru sent an expedition to Easter Island. At this stage, the local population was estimated to number approximately 3,000. However, when British navigator Sir James Cook arrived four years later, there were only around 600 to 700 men and around 30 women living in the island. The island's population received further setbacks after slave trade raids (known as "blackbirding"), as well as a smallpox epidemic, reduced the population to just over 100 by 1877.

In 1888, Easter Island was annexed to Chile and the land was used mostly for raising sheep. Finally, by 1966 the residents were recognised as Chilean citizens, and started to gain some ability to self-determine.

Easter Island has now a population of around 3,300 people of mixed ancestry. The prevalent ethnicity still remains Polynesian. The island was declared a UNESCO World Heritage site in 1996, and its principal economic activity is tourism.

 75mm, f/11, ISO 50, 1/5 sec
FF camera

1.64 The setting sun over Ahu Tahai is a popular picnic venue at the end of the day.

Index of locations

Walkabout photo guides

About us

Walkabout photo guides was founded with the express mission of enabling budding travel photographers to get out and explore new places and come home with great photos. We combine experience on the ground with extensive research, distilling it into a coherent structure, saving the reader hours of time. Our guides enable the reader to confidently be on top of the logistics of a trip focused on taking photos (which is often different to a holiday).

No matter whether you're a weekend warrior, digital nomad, or first-time traveller, our guides will shortcut a lot of the planning and logistics that can stand in the way of getting great travel photos.

About the author

James Dugan was born and raised in Australia. The travel bug bit him on his first trip overseas to India aged 13. Photography became a passion early on as a way of capturing his travels, and as a creative outlet to balance against corporate life. It also became a way to inspire and encourage others, stuck in their cubicles, to get out and explore. This guide draws on these experiences and paying forward the help and support received over the years.